All Wool

W. C. Tuttle

Alpha Editions

This edition published in 2024

ISBN : 9789366386171

Design and Setting By
Alpha Editions
www.alphaedis.com
Email - info@alphaedis.com

As per information held with us this book is in Public Domain.
This book is a reproduction of an important historical work. Alpha
Editions uses the best technology to reproduce historical work in the same
manner it was first published to preserve its original nature. Any marks or
number seen are left intentionally to preserve its true form.

Contents

ALL WOOL...- 1 -

ALL WOOL

By W. C. Tuttle

Author of "A Bull Movement in Yellow Horse,"

"Psychology and Copper," etc.

Zeb Whitney laid the ace of diamonds down on the rock and grinned at Ricky Saunders.

"Go on, Ricky. Play that li'l ol' jack. I got high, low, and that jack will jist put me out. That'll make fifty thousand yuh owe me and——"

Ricky laid his cards on the rock and peered over Zeb's shoulder.

"Look at that sheep, Zeb! What do yuh reckon ails him?"

"Never mind th' sheep," replied Zeb. "Yuh can't git me to turn around so yuh can eat that jack. Go on, play it."

"I tell yuh somethin's wrong," insisted Ricky. "That sheep jist turned uh flip-flop and he ain't got up since."

"Mebby that's th' way sheeps do," remarked Zeb. "Yuh see me and you ain't been nursin' sheep but uh short time and we ain't hep to all their proclivities."

Ricky sat down and picked up his cards. "I'd shore like to know what hit that sheep. Honest, he jist——"

Sping!

A bullet ricocheted off the rock they were using for a card-table and whined off down across the foothills.

"Duck!" yelled Zeb, as he went crabwise down the opposite side of the rock and slid around behind the stunted pine tree which had shaded their seven-up game.

"Come down here, yuh blamed mutt!" he stormed at Ricky, who sat there looking at the scratch on the rock where the bullet had glanced. "Ain't yuh got no sense a tall?"

"What was it, Zeb?" inquired Ricky innocently, as he slid down beside Zeb and pulled out his papers and tobacco.

"Somebody was shootin' at us," stated Zeb. "And danged good shootin' too if anybody should ask yuh."

Ricky shaped his cigaret and fumbled for a match.

"Say, Zeb, I wonder if them same jaspers didn't hit that sheep? By golly! I'll bet that was it. Mebby—aw say, Zeb, if that was uh rifle-bullet why don't we hear th' report?"

Zeb smiled patronizingly and relieved Ricky of his tobacco.

"Ricky, them high-power rifles kin shoot three miles, and they don't make much noise a-tall. At this distance yuh wouldn't hear it a tall, *sabe?*"

Ricky got up and climbed back on the rock. He gazed off in the direction from which the bullet had come and then sat down and began dealing the cards.

"Come on up, Zeb," he urged. "Three miles is uh long ways to see uh target and th' man who can hit me at that distance is plumb welcome to cut uh notch on his gunstock, and besides it's too danged hot out there in th' sun."

Zeb climbed back and sat down against the tree.

"Ricky, I plumb wish we hadn't taken this job."

"Unha," agreed Ricky, intent on his solitaire layout.

"Yes, sir, I am," continued Zeb. "I knowed something was wrong when Jim Watts offers us uh hundred apiece uh month to dry nurse these darn animated wool gardens. Ricky, uh hundred dollars uh month is too much money to pay uh sheep-herder. Didn't yuh ever notice it?"

Ricky laid down the cards and laughed.

"Too much? Why, Zeb, I'd herd sheep for uh million dollars uh month. Honest, there ain't no large amount uh money that would be too big to tempt me to herd sheep."

"Ricky," pronounced Zeb, "yo're as funny as th' dobie itch. No man pays that price unless thar's uh mighty good reason."

Ricky swept up the cards and put them in his pocket, and then settled himself comfortably.

"Zeb Whitney, every day is th' first of April to you. If I was as suspicious as you are I'd git arrested. Jist because we're uh long ways from home and in uh strange land, and cause uh feller likes our looks and gives us uh job takin' care of his woolen meal-tickets at so much per care, you immediately and soon gits th' idea that there's uh brick under th' hat. Look at th' doughnut fer uh while, Zeb, and quit lookin' at th' hole in th' center."

Zeb shook his head solemnly.

"Did yuh notice that there ain't no dogs connected with this outfit? Did yuh notice how scared that greaser was when we come and how quick he rolled his blankets and beat it? And also did yuh notice," he continued before Ricky had a chance to reply, "that Watts said he would give us a fat bonus if we kept th' herd here for two months?"

"What's th' answer?" yawned Ricky.

"Sheep war."

"Haw! Haw!" laughed Ricky. "Sheep war, eh? Who are th' sheep goin' to fight?

By golly, Zeb, if these sheep want to start anything I'll——"

"Have uh little sense!" growled Zeb. "Listen. I seems to remember readin' uh few weeks ago about trouble brewin' between th' sheep and cattle men some place—believe I reads it in th' Breeder's magazine."

"Uh course this would have to be th' place," replied Ricky sarcastically. "Yuh don't remember where it was, Zeb, but this shore must be it. Trouble jist simply stalks in yore footsteps—curses!"

"Well, anyway," stated Zeb, "Watts will be back here in uh couple uh weeks with fresh grub and then I'll have uh li'l heart-to-heart talk with him."

"Yes, and jist about git into an argument with him and lose us our jobs. Let's haze them burr catchers back to camp and git some grub."

The hazing part was easier said than done. It had been easy to let the herd wander away from the bed ground in the cool of the morning but it was a different task to round up three thousand sheep in the evening without the aid of dogs and herd them back to the shelter of the little valley. Ricky and Zeb were cow-punchers by nature, and this walking and running after sheep was not by any means delightful. It was dark when they got back to camp and both were fagged out.

"Now, I reckon you'll remark that uh hundred uh month is too much pay, eh?" exploded Ricky, as he threw himself down on a blanket inside the tent and nursed a sore hip where an excited ram had hit him on the run. "Touch off that fire and let's git something to eat."

The fire had been laid since morning. Zeb, knowing that in all probabilities they would both be tired when night came, had thoughtfully laid a fire in the sheet-iron stove before leaving.

"Take that bucket and git some water from th' spring," ordered Zeb. "And don't forget to strain th' wool out of it before yuh comes back."

"I don't know where it is," wailed Ricky. "I never saw any spring. Watts showed you where it was but I was up here all th' time watchin' that greaser. Come on and show me where it is, Zeb. I'd shore admire uh nice cool drink from th' wool-covered bucket that hung in th' well."

Zeb grumbled while he lit the fire and then picked up the bucket.

"Come on and I'll show yuh our water supply."

They went out of the tent and scrambled down the bank of a deep washout behind the tent.

"Don't slide into it," warned Zeb.

"Aw, slide yer grandmother!" retorted Ricky. "Any time I slide you can——"

Ricky failed to state just what he would do in case he did happen to slide, for at that certain moment the whole world seemed to fly up and hit them in the face and they both flopped head first into the spring. A few seconds later something sailed down and lit with a loud smash in the bottom of the washout.

"Gi-gi-git yer darned boots out of my mouth!" gurgled Ricky. "What do yuh think my face is—uh welcome mat?"

"What in the name of seven kinds of purgatory was that?" mumbled Zeb, wiping the water and mud out of his mouth.

"Swallered all th' water, ate all th' wool and had uh boot-heel for uh chaser," announced Ricky drunkenly.

"What in thunder hit in th' washout?" asked Zeb.

"I ought to know," replied Ricky sarcastically. "Unha, I reckon I ought to know, bein' as I was under about seven feet uh alkali water with yore boots in my mouth."

"I heard it hit," stated Zeb.

"Unha," agreed Ricky. "Sounded like uh hardware store done leaped before it looked. Let's go back to th' tent and see what happened."

They climbed back up the bank and started for the tent, when Zeb grabbed Ricky by the arm and gasped in astonishment.

"Where?" he whispered.

Ricky rubbed a muddy hand across his eyes.

"She ain't," he remarked inanely. "Zeb, she's done went away."

"Giant powder!" exclaimed Zeb, sniffing the air. "Somebody done put dinnamite in our stove, Ricky!"

Ricky walked around the hole in the ground where the tent had stood.

"Tent's gone," he announced foolishly. "Good-by tent! Jerusalem! Zeb, our grub is all gone, too! Blewed up. Rifle gone, too, and—say, Zeb, you got yore six-gun—unha, yo're gun's safe but mine was on th' grub-box."

"Sheeps gone too," stated Zeb.

"Blew—aw, what do we care. I reckon they heard th' noise and hit fer th' hills. What do we care for th' sheep, eh?"

"Blankets gone," groaned Zeb. "Nothin' to eat and no place to sleep. Now mebby you'll agree with me that this ain't no white man's job, Ricky."

"Man size, anyway," replied Ricky, sitting down and rolling a cigaret.

Zeb watched him in silence until the smoke was made and then an idea seemed to strike him:

"How much smokin' yuh got on yore person, Ricky?"

Ricky held up a limp sack containing about two more cigarets.

"And I ain't got uh bit," stated Zeb. "She was all in that defunct grub-box."

"Well," remarked the philosophical Ricky, "they can't blow our camp up no more. It ain't as though they had only blew up part of it. Golly, Zeb, I'm shore hungry! What about uh little supper, eh? Give me yore gun and I'll see if I can pick uh fat blatter in th' dark while you builds uh little fire, eh?"

"She tastes to me like it was uh sinful waste uh lead," stated Ricky about an hour later, as he raked a piece of half-cooked

- 6 -

meat out of the coals. "Doggone it, Zeb, uh sheep ought to be raised fer wool exclusive. As uh tender morsel I opines that she runs uh dead heat with owls and rawhide. Pass th' salt please."

Zeb threw a piece of smoking meat at Ricky's head and rolled over on the ground.

"Ricky, what are we goin' to do? Will we roll out of here and let th' sheep nurse themselves or will we stay here until Watts comes or until we starve to death? Golly, he can't blame us if we do leave. What yuh say?"

"Leavin' all jokin' aside, Zeb, jist what does this all mean?" asked Ricky. "Got any real idea, Zeb?"

"Sheep war," stated Zeb. "Or at any rate I believes she is. I takes it that th' cattlemen here are uh heap sore at th' sheep and wants to drive 'em all off th' range. I reads it all in that article back in Blue Joint. I reckon that is why we gits this job so easy. Watts ain't got no other place to range his woolies and he's plumb got to have herders. Greasers won't put up no fight a-tall, and so he pays uh big salary to white men to guard his property, *sabe*? I figgers it that some of th' hangers-on of th' cattlemen done went and loaded our stove with giant powder and takes uh chance that we'll git elevated so much that we won't look at no sheep-herdin' job no more, Ricky. That's uh dirty mucker trick I takes it."

"Unha," agreed Ricky. "I shore hates to quit in uh case like that. Mebby we'll starve or go crazy and start blattin' like uh pair uh two-legged woolies, Zebbie, old top but I'm game to sit in th' game for uh few days yet. What say?"

They solemnly shook hands across their little fire and then Ricky produced that greasy deck of cards again.

"Doggone yo're hide," he drawled, "I'll play yuh to see if she's uh hundred thousand or quits. That last jack wasn't le-gitimate, Zeb. It's got uh corner torn and yuh knowed it."

The next three days were a nightmare of chasing sheep through the dust and heat and then eating half-cooked mutton for breakfast, dinner and supper, and of sleeping on the bare ground with nothing but the sky for a blanket. It gets cool in the small hours of the morning in the range country, albeit the thermometer rises to the century mark in the shade at midday.

During that time they had glimpses of cowboys riding across the upper part of the range but there had been no further demonstrations of violence.

On the morning of the fourth day it was a gaunted, sorrowful pair of shepherds who trailed that big bunch of sheep out of the valley and up the hills. Zeb strode in the lead and hurled imprecations on all wool-bearing animals, as one old ram detached himself from the band and tried to go back to the bed ground.

"'At a boy!" yelled Ricky, as Zeb bounced a piece of basalt rock off the ram's head. "Git back yuh old curly horned animated bock-beer sign!" he whooped as the ram lowered its head and dove for him.

Ricky made a frantic effort to escape, and although the ram failed to hit him square they both went down in a heap and rolled down the hill. Zeb forgot his peeve in the excitement and doubled up with mirth.

"Haw! Haw! Haw!" roared a strange voice, as Ricky succeeded in getting on top of the ram. "Haw! Haw! Pretty good for uh shepherd."

Zeb turned and faced three cowboys on horseback, who had ridden up unnoticed. They slouched in their saddles and grinned at Ricky's efforts to choke the ram. Ricky kicked the ram in the ribs and then limped up to where Zeb was.

"Haw! Haw!" mimicked Ricky in a sneering tone. "I knowed uh jackass oncet which had uh voice like that and also about th' same idea of humor."

"Sweet-tempered little shepherd, ain't he?" laughed one of the punchers. "Eatin' raw sheep meat ain't calmed his disposition none whatever."

"I likes 'em raw," stated Ricky. "I also like cow-punchers when they're not too raw, but they're usually uh little too light fer uh man-sized re-past."

"That's uh plenty," snarled the one at whom Ricky had seemingly been making his remarks. "We never came over here to exchange pleasantries with shepherds. We're here to tell yuh to move yore woolies off this range right now, *sabe?* Tonight is th' night. After this there ain't goin' to be no more sheep on th' Willow Creek range. If you won't move 'em, we will, *sabe?*"

"You fellers," drawled Ricky, "reminds me of dynamite in uh tin stove. It makes uh lot uh noise and messes up uh lot uh good grub and—oh well, if yuh don't want to hear what I think of yuh, jist keep on goin'," he remarked, as the three turned their horses and galloped off across the hills.

"Well, what do yuh know about that?" groaned Zeb. "I reckon tonight is th' night we move, Ricky."

"Unha," agreed Ricky. "I reckon yore right. Dang bust the luck! I sprained my thumb on that old ram. Wow! She shore hurts."

Zeb shoved his hands down in his overall pockets and frowned at the sun.

"It's twenty miles to Mill City, Ricky. Did yuh ever think about what a walk that is?"

"Gosh, uh sore thumb is terrible, Zeb!" wailed Ricky. "I ain't in no shape to walk a tall now. Twenty miles! Gee, Zeb, I never did nor never will walk that far with my insides cryin' out fer grub th' way they are right now. I reckon I've plumb lost my appetite."

"I'm gittin' sorta finicky myself," agreed Zeb. "I don't seem to look upon uh piece uh sheep meat th' way uh hungry man should."

A continuous repast of mutton and salt is almost sure to make even the best of digestive apparatus go awry. They had eaten it roasted in the coals, baked in clay, boiled in the water bucket and fried on a piece of the sheet-iron stove which had survived the explosion. The morning meal had been thrown away untasted.

That day they laid in the shade of the lone pine tree, too miserable to even play seven-up. At dinner-time they grinned and pulled up another notch on their belts. Both of them were inveterate cigaret-smokers—or rather had been until, as Ricky remarked:

"Dynamite is uh sure cure fer th' cigaret habit, Zeb. She cures but she don't remove th' cravin'."

That night they wended their weary way back to the bed ground and left the sheep out on the range. They had decided that there was no reason for bringing in the herd. If the cattlemen were bent on chasing them out of the country, why not let them have the trouble of rounding them up?

"Want some boiled mutton?" asked Ricky, after they had thrown their tired bodies down on the ground above the spring.

Zeb sat up and reached for a rock but the effort was too much and he flopped down again.

"Ricky," he murmured, "if I ever gits my strength back again— I hates to do it, Ricky—but I'm goin' to massacree you."

Ricky got up painfully and built a little fire.

"She seems more homelike thataway, Zeb. If I passes out I shore don't want to do it in th' dark. Judas Priest, I wish I had uh smoke."

"Old man Lute was uh goldarned brute, and he couldn't git his longhorns up th' goldarned chute," sang Zeb, in a low mournful voice. "I wonder if they're bluffin' or if they really means to hold uh party down here tonight?"

"I ain't got uh danged thing to wear," wailed Ricky. "My tailor done told me this mornin': 'Mr. Saunders, I can't possibley git that swaller-tailed——'"

"*Sh-h-h-h!*" cautioned Zeb, sitting up and grasping Ricky by the sleeve. "Listen! Hear anything?"

A faint tinkle like the light tap of metal on stone sounded from up the washout, and was immediately followed by a smothered exclamation.

Zeb rolled over and slid feet first down the washout and pulled Ricky with him just as a bullet ploughed through their little fire and a streak of orange flame flashed further up the gully. Zeb ducked low and started up the washout in the direction of the gun-flash.

"Where yuh goin'?" whispered Ricky, trailing along behind.

"Keep down low," commanded Zeb. "We got to git in behind 'em. Come on and keep quiet."

They sneaked along for a few hundred yards when Zeb stopped and peered over the bank.

"I got it all figgered out, Ricky. Them jaspers never walked over to th' party. It's all of seven miles to th' nearest cow-camp. I'm figgerin' that they—look out! Git down low!"

"What yuh see?"

"Jist what I expected. Them jaspers done left their hosses over by that bunch of cottonwoods. Look! See it?"

"See what?"

"Come on, Ricky, and keep down low. They've left one feller over there with th' hosses and, Ricky, he's smokin' uh real cigaret!"

"Uh cigaret," murmured Ricky. "Mama mine, I'd spank uh female grizzly's cub in th' ol' lady's presence for one long drag on uh cigaret. Ouch—gol dang——"

"*Sh-h-h-h!*" sibilated Zeb.

"Aw—if you'd got yer knees in uh cactus patch you'd say *sh-h-h-h!*" retorted Ricky in an undertone.

They sneaked around behind the patch of cottonwoods and in behind the four horses. Those range-bred horses made no move except to nuzzle Ricky as he whispered—

"Steady li'l bronks."

The cowboy sat on his heels some distance in front of the horses and puffed away at his cigaret. Ricky got one good whiff of that cigaret and then took one long step and dove straight for the unsuspecting cowboy. Ricky's right arm described a short arc as he plunged, and the cowboy rolled over without a sound.

Ricky got up and rolled him over and felt of his heart.

"Fine work!" he exclaimed. "That loaded quirt I took off that saddle was jist th' thing, Zeb. Look what I got."

He held up a sack of tobacco and a book of cigaret-papers.

"And that ain't all either," he continued. "I found this roll uh bills in th' same pocket and——"

"Ricky, we ain't thieves," stated Zeb.

"Not any," agreed Ricky. "But, Zeb, this ain't stealin'. Somebody's got to pay th' freight, and it's uh cinch that I ain't goin' to search fer Watts to collect uh few days' pay. We simply got to have uh little money and if it eases yore mind any, Zeb, you can consider this my money, *sabe?*"

"They're comin' back, Ricky!"

Loud voices raised in a heated argument floated across the sage-brush flat and coming closer all the time.

"You take that big roan, Ricky, and I'll take th' black. Slip th' bridles off the other two and cut their cinches."

It was but a moment's work to slip the rigs off the extra horses, and then they mounted and moved off slowly in the shadow of the trees until they were behind the cottonwoods. Suddenly there was a shout from the cowboys and they knew their work had been discovered. Ricky pulled up his big roan and turned in the saddle.

"Walk, dang yuh, walk!" he yelled at the top of his voice and then, spurring their horses, they streaked off across the moonlit foothills in the general direction of Mill City, followed by a scattering volley of pistol-shots and unprintable remarks.

It was noon the next day when they rode into the little town of Mill City. They had taken the wrong road and had ridden miles out of their way before they met a person who set them on the right trail. They rode up in front of a Chinese restaurant and Ricky handed his reins to Zeb and slid painfully to the ground.

"I'll order everything he's got," he announced. "You put them horses in a stable some place and hurry back. Gosh, I'm starved plumb to death."

Zeb rode on up the street to the one livery-stable. He was too hungry and tired to take off the saddles so he left the horses outside.

"Unsaddle 'em and give 'em uh good feed," he ordered the stable man, and then started back to the restaurant.

He had almost reached the door when he saw Ricky come out, propelled by a big bearded person, who whirled his partner around roughly and started down the street, shoving him by the shoulder. Ricky was protesting loudly and already several people were walking curiously toward them. Zeb quickened his pace until he was walking at Ricky's side.

"What's th' trouble?" he asked.

- 13 -

"I'm arrested, that's all!" exclaimed Ricky, and Zeb, acting on the spur of the moment and without any preliminary windup, whirled and smashed the officer on the jaw with his right.

The officer dropped like a rock. It was a clean knock-out. Zeb gave him one look and then grabbed Ricky by the arm.

"Come on!" he yelled. "Run, you son-of-a-gun, run! We've got to git to them hosses quick!"

He dashed off down the dusty street and Ricky pounded along behind. Several people on the street had seen the blow struck but they made no move to stop the pair. The suddenness of it all and the limp form of the officer lying there on the board sidewalk drew their attention more than did the two dust-covered figures racing for the livery-stable.

"Pure bull luck!" panted Zeb. "Them hosses ain't been unsaddled yet. "Git a-goin'!" he yelled as he climbed into the saddle and spurred the black around the corner.

Ricky needed no urging. His big roan was right on the heels of the black when they hit the down grade toward Sweet Grass Valley.

Not a word was spoken until they had put at least a dozen miles between them and Mill City. At the forks of the road, Zeb pulled up and turned in his saddle.

"Which one do yuh reckon th' posse will take in case they hit our trail, Ricky?"

Ricky rolled a smoke and scratched his head foolishly.

"I don't reckon it makes much difference which one we take," he remarked. "They ain't goin' to foller us far. Hittin' uh deputy ain't no hangin' matter, Zeb."

"No, but hoss stealin' is," reminded Zeb seriously.

"Who said anything about horse stealin'?" demanded Ricky.

Zeb squinted his eyes and looked Ricky over carefully from heels to hat.

"Say, Ricky, jist about what in the devil did that feller arrest yuh for?"

"Hittin' uh Chinaman," chuckled Ricky, between puffs.

"Hittin' uh Chinaman!" exploded Zeb. "What fer?"

"Zeb—" Ricky leaned over and put his hand on Zeb's shoulder and a humorous light twinkled in his gray eyes—"I hadn't no more than sat down in that restaurant until one uh them danged slant-eyed celestials comes over to me and says, 'You likee some nice roast mutton?'"

Zeb reached over and shook hands solemnly with Ricky and then turned his horse down the left-hand fork of the road.

"Ricky," he laughed, "'let's git a-goin'. This country is all wool but she ain't wide enough fer me and you."

THE END

- 16 -

www.ingramcontent.com/pod-product-compliance
Ingram Content Group UK Ltd.
Pitfield, Milton Keynes, MK11 3LW, UK
UKHW031833270325
456796UK00003B/483